I0427012

PROP-TRADING: HOW TO MAKE MONEY ON FINANCIAL MARKETS WITH MINIMAL RISKS

PRACTICAL RECOMMENDATIONS ON PROPRIETARY TRADING IN THE FOREX AND FUTURES MARKET

WARNING OF RISKS

Trading any financial instrument including currencies, futures, stocks or cryptocurrencies has a high profit potential, but also involves a high risk of capital loss. Before you begin you must recognize this risk and be prepared to accept it. None of the information below is a guarantee that you will receive funds to manage. All information described is intended to be used for educational and research purposes. The author of the guide assumes no responsibility for the consequences of the financial decisions you make.

CONTENTS

INTRODUCTION

This manual was created to provide traders with concentrated information about the essence of prop trading, its advantages and disadvantages. The manual does not contain trading training, guaranteed algorithms and trading strategies, but the information presented is enough to pass the selection process and receive a trading deposit for management in any prop-trading company.

50% of information is available in open sources, 50% is personal experience of trial and error. If you have 3-6 months of «unnecessary» time and «unnecessary» 2.000-3.000$ - all this can be found and learned by yourself. Buying this book, you save your time and money, moreover you can start earning well. Everything depends only on you.

These practical recommendations will be relevant:
 - for beginners or just learning trading and thinking about where to get money for a trading deposit;
 - for trading traders who do not have sufficient trading capital;
 - for experienced traders as an opportunity to scale their income.

Some traders have a negative attitude towards proprietary trading, arguing that proprietary companies are poorly controlled, are located in offshore zones, and do not take your trades to the real market. But, what do we care about all this if the company has been on the market for several years and has been consistently paying out profits. If it was a loss making business or illegal, I doubt they would take such a risk. Yes, of course, there are fraudulent companies, but they are isolated and for this there is diversification by prop-companies. I will tell you how to do it right next.

WHAT IS PROP-TRADING?

Prop-trading is an investment business model in which a company with capital transfers a portion of its assets to hired traders to trade on exchanges under certain conditions. Large funds and companies are engaged in prop-trading. The basis of the work of proprietary trading companies is the constant search and hiring of traders who are offered capital to carry out trading transactions without the need to use their own funds. The income generated is shared between the company and the trader. The company is interested in attracting successful traders who will quickly and efficiently increase their capital and with it the company's capital. That being said, proprietary companies also want to see that you abide by the principles of risk management and can follow the rules.

So, the general sense of this business for a trader is as follows: to get a deposit in management in the amount of let's say 25.000$, it is necessary to pass the selection, for which you need to pay an average of 150-200$. The selection consists of test trading on a demo account. As a rule, all companies have selection programmes in one stage, in two stages and some in three stages. If it is a one-stage programme, you need to earn usually 10% of your deposit, after that you will be given a trading account to manage. If it is a two-stage programme, you need to earn usually 8-10% of your deposit in the first stage and 4-5% of your deposit in the second stage. How much time is usually not set. On a three-stage programme you will need to earn the required amount three times. All companies have different conditions on the total drawdown and drawdown per day, here you need to study their conditions, we will talk about it further.

As a rule, all companies offer trading accounts of 5.000$, 10.000$, 25.000$, 50.000$, 100.000$, 200.000$, 300.000$. Accordingly, the price for passing the selection process will be different depending on the size of the deposit you want to manage.

It should be understood that this deposit amount is conditional. You will have purchasing power for this amount, but you can usually lose only 10%. Trading on your own deposit, you can go into a drawdown even at minus 50%, but in a proprietary company you will not be allowed to do so.

After passing the selection process and receiving a deposit for management, you trade as your own money. The profit made is divided in the ratio of 70-90% to you and the rest to the company. Trading very conservatively and earning 5% per month, from this deposit you can get every month at least $1.000. And if it is a deposit of $100.000 or $500.000, count for yourself. The first time you make a profit your screening money is refunded.

My opinion - this is a very profitable business, most importantly you do not risk your money.

CONCEPTUAL FRAMEWORK

Here are the basic terms you need to know to understand prop-trading and get selected for a prop-company.

Challenge - is the process of testing a trader's trading skills. It can also be called a test, evaluation program, selection.

Fee, One-time fee or Refundable fees (registration fee) - is a payment for the right to pass the Challenge. It is paid to the proprietary company, in most cases in case of successful completion of the Challenge this fee is returned to the trader during the first payment.

Account size - the amount of the deposit on which the Challenge is held. After successful completion, this is the deposit you will receive for management.

Profit target - the amount of profit after which you are considered to have passed the Challenge stage. It is usually specified as a percentage of the account size or a specific amount.

Maximum loss - the total amount of loss received when completing a Challenge. Usually, it is 10% of the account size or a specific amount specified by the company. If it is reached, the Challenge is considered as not passed. It can be static or dynamic. It is always indicated in your personal cabinet. The current loss is taken into account. For example, you have a deposit of 10.000$, the maximum allowed drawdown of 1.000$, you have made a trade, and the price goes against you, if you achieve a loss of -1.000$ or more, regardless of whether it is fixed or the transaction is not closed yet, you will violate this rule and fail the selection or lose the account.

Maximum daily loss - allowable amount of loss during a day. As a rule, it is 5% of the account size or a specific amount specified by the company. If it is reached, the Challenge is considered as not passed. It can be static or dynamic. It is calculated each time anew from the balance or equity at the beginning of the day. It is better to see it in your personal cabinet and take it into account when calculating stop losses.

Minimum trading days - the minimum number of days for which you can reach the profit goal. If according to the terms of the Challenge there are 5 of them, and you have reached the goal for 3 days, you still need to trade 2 more days to fulfill the conditions, usually you can with a minimum lot. A trading day is counted if at least one trade was opened and closed on that day. If you opened a trade on Monday and closed it on Wednesday and did not trade on Tuesday, it will be counted as one trading day. This information allows you to calculate the minimum time you are allowed to complete the Challenge.

Time limit or Trading period - the maximum number of days to reach the profit target. Usually, 30 or 60 days. If the goal is not reached during this period, the Challenge is considered not passed. Now many companies remove limits on passing.

Profit split - the ratio of how much of the profit earned is paid to the trader and how much is left to the company.

Max capital - the maximum amount of deposit or the sum of several deposits, which can be managed by one trader.

First withdrawal - after how many days the trader can receive payments of the received profit. All companies have different, mostly from 5 to 30 days. If this information is not openly specified, you should look in the FAQ section of the site.

Drawdown type - an algorithm for calculating deposit drawdown. There are Traling Drawdown on equity, Equity/Balance, Balance Based.

Traling Drawdown is always counted from the current funds on the trading account taking into account even the profit on open deals in real time. The principle is similar to trailing stop. For example, you have a balance at the beginning of the day of 10.000$, the maximum daily drawdown (dynamic) is equal to 500$. You make a deal, the price goes in your direction, and the maximum profit on the open deal is 600$, i.e. you had 10.600$ on your account. Then the price turns around and you need to take into account that the drawdown starts to be counted from this amount, i.e. when the balance reaches 10.100$ you will reach the maximum daily drawdown. I categorically do not recommend companies where dynamic drawdown is applied.

Equty/Balance is calculated from the balance or current funds on the trading account, whichever is greater. It is updated once a day.

Balance Based is calculated from the balance of the trading account at the beginning of the day.

For example, your balance at the beginning of the day is 10.000$, the maximum daily drawdown (static) is 500$. That is, you will reach the maximum daily drawdown when your deposit reaches $9.500, no matter what the maximum profit was before.

Scaling - an opportunity provided by the company to increase the size of your trading deposit.

Consystency rules - company terms and conditions that regulate or restrict a trader's trading. For example, whether it is allowed to transfer trading positions through the night or weekends, whether it is allowed to trade on news, whether it is allowed to use Expert Advisors, allowed maximum daily profit, maximum position size and other. It is indicated openly on the site or in the FAQ section of the site. It is necessary to know them, because if you violate them, you can lose your account, regardless of whether it is the period of the Challenge or already trading on a real account.

ADVANTAGES AND DISADVANTAGES OF PROP-TRADING

What is the benefit of the trading company itself? It is that it receives a part of the profit from each successful trade of a trader. That is, the longer and more successful a trader trades, the higher the company's income. As a rule, a trader who has passed the selection process and received an account for management is first observed by the company's specialists and, if the trader trades in plus and has adequate risk management, the company starts copying his trades and earns even more.

Advantages of trading in a proprietary company:

1) Trading deposit. Prop-trading has one important advantage, it is an opportunity to earn on the market without risking your own money. A trader trading through a broker always risks his money. It is also attractive for traders who do not have sufficient financial capacity. The smaller the deposit, the harder it is for a trader to make money, so many people choose to trade with a proprietary company. At the same time, the cost of completing the Challenge is affordable for the average trader.

2) Discipline, a system of risk and money management. A trader cannot lose money in one day or in one trade. The company limits risks within a trading day and sets limits of possible losses. This disciplines the trader. Also, sufficient capital for trading reduces the trader's risk in one trade.

3) Community. Prop-companies often gather traders in Telegram, Skype or Discord, where traders can trade together, analyze trading tools, confer, predict some situations. This improves the quality of trading.

4) Opportunity to get a large capital to manage. The company constantly analyzes traders' activity. If you are a promising trader with good trading statistics, you can get a capital much larger than the initial one in the prop-company.

5) Since you are an employee, you do not need to register, inform or declare your deposits in foreign financial companies to your competent government authorities because the money does not belong to you.

6) Unlike brokers, proprietary trading companies cannot make money from the financial losses of their clients. In this case, there is no conflict of interest. A proprietary company is interested in your earnings, as it receives a percentage from each profitable trade.

7) Prop-companies themselves choose a broker, through whom traders then trade. And they approach it much more professionally than an ordinary trader.

8) For novice traders, trading with a proprietary company can be the best, and for some, the only way to increase their capital. Moreover, it can be done more safely than in the case of trading solely on one's own funds.

9) Payment for passing the selection, and then the withdrawal of the received profit can be made with cryptocurrency.

Disadvantages of prop-trading:

1) The risk of falling into a fraudulent prop-company, which earns money from traders' registration fees. Thus, it is interested in your failure to pass the Challenge and will interfere in every possible way or will refuse to pay you later.

2) Bankruptcy of the proprietary company. The prop-trading industry is not yet regulated enough to protect traders from this.

3) You will have to work on the software that the company presents. But this is more of an inconvenience than a disadvantage.

4) You may be refused on territorial grounds. Some companies do not co-operate with citizens of certain countries.

TYPES OF PROPRIETARY TRADING COMPANIES

Conventionally, they can be categorized into:

1) those working only on Forex and cryptocurrencies, they are the majority;

2) working only in the futures market;

3) working only on the stock market.

These companies are then divided into providing money to the management:

1) only after completing the challenge;

2) without completing the challenge.

PRACTICAL RECOMMENDATIONS FOR SELECTING A PROP-COMPANY

Before you start the selection process, assess your capabilities so that you don't lose time and money at the selection stage. Remember that selection is paid, but if the result is successful, the company returns your money to you. So, let's start the selection process:

1) Decide on which market you will trade: stocks, forex, futures or crypto.

2) Browse through the websites of the selected prop-companies and compare the conditions for completing the challenge. It is better to choose the standard two-stage shuttles from the evaluation programmes provided by the company. On accelerated programmes or with less requirements for the conditions of passage, as a rule, will be worse trading conditions or more expensive cost. Study the terms of the Challenges by the terms that are explained in the conceptual apparatus.

3) Pay attention to the site itself, it should be modern, informative, not slow. Photos of real people, links to reviews, information about the address of registration, links to accounts in social networks, to be in several languages are desirable. That is, it should be a site that should give the impression that its development and maintenance is allocated normal funding.

4) Be sure to study the trading rules set by the company. Especially pay attention to those conditions, violation of which will lead to account blocking.

Take time to study the section with answers to frequently asked questions. If the rules established by the company interfere with your trading style or violate your trading strategy, you should also refuse such companies.

5) Read reviews in social networks, if the account owner openly talks about his experience of trading in a trading company, demonstrates payments, gives recommendations, if he has a referral link, it is worth registering through it. It doesn't cost you anything, and you will then be able to clarify some nuances or consult with him.

6) When you have chosen a trading company, write to support and ask whether they work with your country, whether there is a need for verification, and if so, what documents are required. Also, clarify in advance the ways to pay for the selection and how to withdraw profits. In order to avoid unexpected difficulties in the future, it is necessary to find out at the initial stage before purchasing a Challenge.

7) Pay attention to the cost of selection, sometimes with equal conditions some company offers cheaper prices. After studying 10-15 companies you will understand the average price for the Challenge, so a very low price should alert you. Sometimes a company has a low pass-through price, but there are additional fees for activating a funded account after pass-through.

8) Some companies offer an increased refund of your payment for the challenge. They also offer a real payment of a percentage of the virtual profits made during the challenge period. This is a marketing move, but also take it into account, money is not superfluous.

9) Choose companies whose drawdown is considered Balance Based or Equty/Balance. Do not choose companies with dynamic drawdown.

10) Compare the profit target, naturally the lower it is the better for you, but remember that most likely then the cost of screening will be higher or the daily and total risk will be lower. Usually the target is 8-10% in the first stage and 4-5% in the second stage.

11) If you trade intraday or scalper, you can take a Regular account, if you trade medium-term and hold trades for several days, you should definitely choose a Swing account.

12) If you plan to trade using a robot, check in advance with support what types of robots they allow you to use. Also, if you are using Expert Advisors to manage positions, also check whether this is allowed. If you plan to copy trades from another account, agree with the support, there are a lot of restrictions on this issue and each company has different ones.

Applying these recommendations, you need to choose 2-3 proprietary companies by comparing conditions and start working with them according to the strategy recommended below. For your convenience, there is a chart at the end of this book for you to fill out. You can use it to help you choose a proprietary company.

WHICH BROKER TO CHOOSE FROM THE PROP COMPANY'S OFFERINGS

Usually, the choice is limited to 2-3 brokers selected by the prop company itself. So, your choice will depend on what you are trading: currencies, indices, stocks or crypto. Next, compare spreads and swaps, especially spread widening. Compare what it has to trade, whether it has your favorite trading instruments. After comparing these characteristics, choose the best one that suits your trading style. You can find out all this on the broker's website or some proprietary companies place test account details on their website. There are several terminals too, but mostly it is MT 4 or MT 5. It is also at your discretion.

HOW TO REDUCE THE COST OF GOING THROUGH THE SCREENING PROCESS AND EVEN GET THE CHALLENGE FOR FREE?

1) Sign up for their social media, companies have regular promotions and discounts for holidays. Sometimes the discounts are up to 50% of the selection price. Or register through affiliate links, in this case the discount will be 5-10%.

2) Some proprietary companies hold trader contests, take part, it's free, and there are up to 100 or more prizes. As prizes, they give out Challenges for different amounts and real money.

3) A lot of companies organize Challenges for reposts in social networks, guessing quotes or winning games. Pay attention to their Discord channels, it is all published there.

STRATEGY FOR WORKING WITH PROPRIETARY COMPANIES

1) Taking into account the above recommendations, we select the 3 most suitable proprietary companies.

2) Decide on the size of the account you will be qualifying for. Optimally, 10 or 25 thousand is recommended. Even if you have the option of taking an account for 100 or 200k, it's better to start there. All that the prop-company has written and positive reviews are good, but it will be more reliable to see for yourself.

3) You trade according to your strategy and get selected. If you are a beginner or just learning, pay attention to traders who have been trading for a long time and offer their analytics and trading signals for a fee. Pay attention to their publicity, trading experience and proof of trading quality. Using their signals, you can pass the selection process.

4) Having received an account for management, you trade until the first profit. The goal is to reach a profit of 5-10%, after that your risks are levelled. Then withdraw the profit in a convenient way and take the next account. This way you also check the company for withdrawal of money. The average figure for proprietary companies is from a few hours to 5-7 working days. If it is longer, you need to look into what the problem is.

5) On the profit you buy an account for 100 or 200 thousand in the same company and start the selection process.

6) Having been selected for a large account, then you trade as conservatively as possible, earning even 2-3% per month, with three accounts of 100 thousand you will have an income of 6-9 thousand dollars per month. Three accounts are the optimal number, you can have five or more, but it will be more difficult to manage them.

7) Repeat points 2,3,4,5 with the second proprietary company on your list, and then with the third. As a result, your goal is to have trading accounts from 100 thousand and more in several proprietary companies. Even if one of them leaves the market, you will have other accounts from which you can earn. This is diversification by proprietary companies. If you have several trading strategies, it is better to have a separate account for each of them.

8) You can scale your income according to the same scheme, the main thing is not to be greedy, observe risks and diversify constantly. Remember that your accounts in a proprietary company can be merged. In order to merge accounts, they must be of the same type and they must be purchased under the same terms and conditions. You can get more detailed information from their technical support.

PLEASE NOTE

1) Use VPN carefully. If you can't work without it, agree with support. Otherwise your account may be blocked.

2) Be attentive to drawdowns, always calculate the position size and stop loss in order not to exceed the allowable drawdown. Check your calculations with the information from your personal cabinet, but take into account that it is published there with a time delay.

3) Have alternative access to your trading account. For example, if you trade on a desktop computer or laptop, install a trading terminal in your smartphone as well.

4) If you often hold positions for several days, it will be more favorable for you to take the Swap Free feature from a prop company, if there is one. Sometimes a good amount of money comes out that you have to give to the broker. To find out when and how exactly your broker charges swap, it is better to check the contract specifications for the instrument you are trading or contact support in advance.

5) Recently, there have been offers on the internet to do the challenge for you. If you decide to resort to such a service, be sure to consider the following factors:

- often such a service is offered by scammers who take an advance payment from you and that's the end of their services;

- by giving your account to the management of third parties, you run a very high risk of getting under sanctions in the propcompany itself and simply lose your deposit, as most propcompanies prohibit the transfer of data from your account to outsiders, as well as the very management of the account by third parties;

- most importantly, do not forget that passing the Challenge is only the beginning. Further you will have to work really on the same conditions and if you do not have any practical skills, you are guaranteed to fail;

Rather than give money to the side, it is better still try to pass the test yourself, it may not succeed the first time, but you will get a lot of experience.

And do not despair in case of failure! There are traders among us who passed the Challenge with 3, 8 or more times. It's not a big deal. But this experience stays with you forever and the easier it is to work later.

6) Do not lose the entire loss limit per day at once. It is very difficult to recover later and hits the trader's psychological state very hard. The maximum you can afford is 2-2,5% of drawdown per day. And the next day your task should be to recover the previous day's drawdown. If you continue to lose trades, then stop trading. Just stop and that's all.

7) As soon as you get a real trading deposit, reduce risks in each trade and slowly earn a safety cushion. As soon as you have earned money, you can increase risks in trades according to your strategy. And immediately set yourself a restriction that you can trade in minus only this daily safety cushion. It is more conservative, but more reliable, if your trading strategy works.

8) If you plan to use EAs in trading or copy trades, you need to purchase this feature additionally or check with the company whether this is allowed. Proprietary companies do not like EAs scalpers, netters, martingale and round-trip trades.

9) Some proprietary companies block players who are toxic in their opinion, who take excessive risks and constantly break the rules, after a certain period of time the company does not allow them to re-register.

10) If you will withdraw money to the Rise payment system, make sure that the mail address on Rise and the one specified when registering with the propcompany are the same. Otherwise, the money will hang, and you won't be able to understand why for a long time.

11) Almost all prop companies do not have multi-lingual support on their website, usually 1-3 languages. If you don't know the language, you can use a translator, for example one built into your browser.

CONCLUSION

Prop-trading is an excellent choice for those who strive for financial independence. Today it is a unique opportunity for anyone to earn money on financial markets using the capital of a proprietary company. I have tried to concentrate my experience of working with prop-trading companies. Join us! I will also be glad to receive your feedback. To everyone who leaves a review or recommendation, I can save you time and provide a list of verified prop-companies. If you still have questions, write fortradingfx99@gmail.com, I will try to answer all readers.

Success in making money!

Prop	Account size	Max Drawdown	Daily Drawdown	Profit Target	Payout Split	Profit Split Period	News Trading	Swing Trading	EAs Trading	Refund	Withdrawal profit	Price	Promo

Prop	Account size	Max Drawdown	Daily Drawdown	Profit Target	Payout Split	Profit Split Period	News Trading	Swing Trading	EAs Trading	Refund	Withdrawal profit	Price	Promo

Prop	Account size	Max Drawdown	Daily Drawdown	Profit Target	Payout Split	Profit Split Period	News Trading	Swing Trading	EAs Trading	Refund	Withdrawal profit	Price	Promo

Prop	Account size	Max Drawdown	Daily Drawdown	Drawdown type	Profit Target	Payout Split	Profit Split Period	News Trading	Swing Trading	EAs Trading	Withdrawal profit	Price	Promo

FOR NOTES

FOR NOTES

FOR NOTES

www.ingramcontent.com/pod-product-compliance
Lightning Source LLC
Chambersburg PA
CBHW071020290526
45795CB00005B/1875